Dedicated to the victim of victims..

The author has over 25 years of clinical experience in the healthcare field. Is cognisant of both DSM-5-TR (and previous versions) and ICD-11 (and previous versions) disorders and conditions; quality and safety improvement in healthcare; and healthcare education.

"Reflective Thinking: the True Healthcare Tool."
Germany: Hilphma Publications: 2022.

"Burnout in Healthcare."
Germany: Hilphma Publications: 2022.

"Reasonable Resilience in Workplaces and Healthcare Work."
Germany: Hilphma Publications: 2022.

"The Psychological Impacts of Labelling and Failure to Diagnose."
Germany: Hilphma Publications: 2022.

"The Controversy of the Remorseless and Unempathic Healthcare Worker."
Germany: Hilphma Publications: 2023.

"Attitudinal and Personality Traits in the Individual and Healthcare."
Germany: Hilphma Publications: 2023.

"Gaslighting."
Germany: Hilphma Publications: 2023.

CONTENTS

"Psychological manipulation, and abuse, takes many forms but in the context of gaslighting it strips the sufferer to the core- insidiously impacting the victim, often to the point of no return.

The secrecy, tactical manouevres, and seemingly pervasive style of abuse, perpetrated by the gaslighter creates gaslightee entrapment, perceptions of unreality and madness, with many sufferers being psychologically, emotionally, and physically, held in a hostage-like situation.

Much focus has been placed upon intimate partner based gaslighting.
There exists however, a multitude of perpetrations involving friendship, familial, and institutional, gaslighting." (1)

The Gaslighting Victims' Questionnaire (GVQ), and the Gaslighting Victims' Questionnaire- Short form (GVQ- Short form), integrates areas of gaslighting abuse identification: exploitation of trust; manipulation and control; creation of doubt in the victim; isolation; hostage taking like symptoms; interrogation; brainwashing; threats and fear-mongering; splitting; labelling; luring; debasement; toxicity; abandonment issues; and so forth. Symptoms of gaslighting impact include coverage of: hopelessness; (learned) helplessness; anxiety; depression; mental and physical exhaustion; moral injury; intrusive cognitions; trauma, and more. Guidelines and recommendations are incorporated, for both scales, to assist the assessor.

The GVQ, and the GVQ-Short form, is based on M.D. Tophus' 5 Gaslighting Victims' Stages. These are: <u>GHFSA: Grooming; Hostage to cruelty; Fragmentation; revelationary Shock; and, Aftermath</u> (1).

The publication:

Tophus, M.D. Gaslighting, Germany: Hilphma Publications: 2023 is an essential resource for the GVQ, and GVQ-Short form, assessor.

Particularly relevant to this publication, as an additional and supportive resource, are the following M.D. Tophus publications:

"The A to Z of Workplace Bullying: For the Healthcare Professional and Beyond." Germany: Hilphma Publications: 2022.

"Trauma United, Life Defined. A Healthcare Tool for Professionals Across the Globe." Germany: Hilphma Publications: 2022.

"The Psychological Impacts of Labelling and Failure to Diagnose". Germany: Hilphma Publications: 2022.

"Burnout in Healthcare". Germany: Hilphma Publications: 2022.

"The Controversy of the Remorseless and Unempathic Healthcare Worker". Germany: Hilphma Publications: 2023.

"The Unfortunate Healthcare Treater, The Hapless Healthcare Therapist: Narcissistic and Borderline Personality Disorder clients. The Grit." Germany: Hilphma Publications: 2022.

Gaslighting Victims' Questionnaire (GVQ) Assessment Guidelines

The assessor is naturally expected to have gathered some relevant information, about current and historical circumstances, beyond basic personal details-from the client/respondent- prior to the administration of the GVQ.

Assessor eligibility:

The GVQ is to be administered by healthcare, and allied healthcare professionals; and, suitably qualified workers in: domestic violence; human resources/occupational departments or outreach from such; patient safety, and ethics, professionals; trauma specialists; and, family support workers.

Respondent/ Client age range:

The GVQ is appropriate for administration to persons 18 years of age or over
(with a literacy level- verbal comprehension skills- of ages 15 years or over).

GVQ basic details:

It consists of 2 sections.
The first section: 195 items (the subscales are based on the 5 M.D. Tophus GHFSA stages:
Grooming; Hostage to cruelty; Fragmentation; revelationary Shock; and, Aftermath).
The second section: 20 key (plus 1 additional) questions.

<u>**Suitability for Gaslighting types:**</u>

-intimate partnerships (domestic)

-familial

-parental

-work/occupational

-medical

-healthcare environments.

Thus, it is a questionnaire suited to reflect gaslighting in a wide variety of circumstances and environments. For instance, in the case of medical gaslighting, this may correlate with existing transference and counter-transference issues, between patient/client and medical professional/therapist.

<u>**Respondent/client focus:**</u>

When there are multiple identified gaslighters involved, it is necessary for the victim to choose the most extensive of the gaslighters, or a repeat of the questionnaire must be undertaken per key gaslighter.

In the event of history of gaslighting in for example- multiple intimate partnerships, then the victim is required to focus only upon the key gaslighter- the alleged perpetrator in question.

In regards to test administration, and the respondent's answers, if the respondent's alleged gaslighting experience is at a later stage than for instance: grooming, hostage to cruelty, and so forth, then they are to answer each statement related to the earlier stage subscale as in hindsight.

Assessor and administration of subscales:

It is highly recommended that the entire questionnaire, regardless of the respondent's circumstances, be administered.

However, the subscales are to be summed seperately, with recommendations- for example- high scores (red flags) provided for each. The summing of the subscales to a total score is thence undertaken.

Process of administering the GVQ:

Upon introducing the administration of the GVQ, the assessor is to give a brief description of gaslighting to the respondent
(please refer to M.D. Tophus' 'Gaslighting' publication for more), without providing extensive examples of such.

<u>**Clarification of key words:**</u>

The Focal Person, referred to in the questionnaire as 'FP', typically may be an
intimate partner, parent, family member, work colleague/manager, healthcare professional, or other professional.

The inclusion of the word 'connection' in the GVQ is to delineate- for example: friendship; family member relationship;
work collegiality; other (patients, and so forth), as some respondents may associate the word 'relationship'
solely with the 'intimate partner' based meaning.

<u>**Extraneous respondent/client variables for consideration:**</u>

Much is dependent upon the stage of gaslighting victimisation: is it current,
or are they in 'freeze' mode- prolonged hostage to cruelty, or fragmentation, stages or attending in the stage of
revelationary shock- about to leave, or after the fact- the aftermath?

In relation to extraneous variables, there is also the issue of a respondent's traumatic memory loss, detachment, or
dissociative issues. These can affect memory and cause memory deficit (either temporary, or otherwise). So too,
with level of respondent insight into perpetrations of gaslighting.
Client disclosure of previously diagnosed conditions, along with the assessor's observation skills and professional
intuition, may elicit this as a consideration.

Some questions are included specifically to ensure consistency, and reliability, of responses provided.

<u>Additional recommended assessment/s:</u>

Assessment for pre-existing clinical disorders, which may impact the results of the questionnaire (1st section), is recommended in some cases (although, specifics of such may be disclosed/ascertained via the 2nd section administration). This is also relevant for the GVQ- Short form.

Assessment for Acute Stress Disorder, or Post-Traumatic Stress Disorder, may also be necessary following administration of either the GVQ, or the GVQ- Short form.

<u>Reason for administering the GVQ and risk:</u>

The results will reflect for instance- a respondent currently experiencing hostage to cruelty- then further subscale categories' items may not seem relevant. However, an assessor without indepth knowledge of the client and their situation, may find it more appropriate to undertake administration of the entire 5 subscales.

It also very much depends upon the reason for undertaking the GVQ assessment, and the planned use of results gathered. A risk assessment, regardless of high scores/red flags as evidential, needs to be undertaken also- especially in the event of administering of less than 5 subscales.

<u>**Scoring and results:**</u>

The subscale score parameters (low, moderate, high) are set as such to incorporate all
primary gaslighting victimisation types.
These are: personal (intimate; parenting; family members); workplace; patients; and, healthcare environments.

Lower scores (non-red/yellow flags), do not necessarily mean that the victim is sans
current suffering or not in imminent danger. There are multiple variables which can influence a victim's
rating of the statements included in the questionnaire. The importance of experienced, qualified
administrators comes into play as professional prowess requires efficient utilisation of the 1st section results and the 2nd
part of the measurement (the interview).

<u>**During administration of the GVQ, the assessor is required to place a mark/notation for their immediate
reference, against any responses given which trigger a red flag alert.**</u>

<u>**(A 'red flag' is considered to be anything which indicates harm to self or others- including potential for).**</u>

**The assessor must then ask for specific clarification (regarding the red flags' alert responses provided)
from the respondent in the 2nd part of the GVQ.**

A risk assessment and/or immediate intervention, is essential- as per required.

<u>The GASLIGHTING VICTIMS' QUESTIONNAIRE: Section 1 (Scale)</u>

It is to be administered by healthcare, and allied healthcare professionals; and, qualified workers in domestic violence; human resources/occupational departments or outreach from such; patient safety, and ethics, professionals; trauma specialists; and, family support workers

The GVQ is appropriate for 18 years or over (with a literacy level- verbal comprehension skills- of at least 15 years of age).

<u>During administration of the GVQ, the assessor is required to place a mark/notation for their immediate reference, against any responses given which trigger a red flag alert.</u>

<u>(A 'red flag' is considered to be anything which indicates harm to self or others- including potential for).</u>

The assessor may then ask for specific clarification (regarding the red flags' alert responses provided) from the respondent in the 2nd part of the GVQ.

A risk assessment and/or immediate intervention, is essential- as per required.

Please provide the client with the 1-5 rating response scale for visual prompting.

Assessor to say to the respondent:
"Please focus your thoughts and responses on the key person identified, this is referred to as the FP: the focal person, or person of focus"

NAME of CLIENT	
CLIENT'S Date of Birth	
DATE ADMINISTERED	
NAME of ASSESSOR	
ASSESSOR'S RECOMMENDATIONS for FURTHER ASSESSMENT MEASURES/IMMEDIATE INTERVENTION(S)	

<u>GROOMING Subscale:</u>

1/ I receive so many digital messages per day that it is difficult to find time to do anything else.

1	2	3	4	5
Never	Rarely	Sometimes	Often	Always

2/ I am constantly questioned about the decisions I make.

1	2	3	4	5
Never	Rarely	Sometimes	Often	Always

3/ I feel overwhelmed by the amount of detail which I am required to divulge about everyday events

1	2	3	4	5
Never	Rarely	Sometimes	Often	Always

4/ If I fail to meet their (the FP's) demands to reveal all, I fear that they will become upset with me.

1	2	3	4	5
Never	Rarely	Sometimes	Often	Always

5/ There is one rule for him/her and another rule for me.

1	2	3	4	5
Never	Rarely	Sometimes	Often	Always

6/ He/she determines the rules for our discussions.

1	2	3	4	5
Never	Rarely	Sometimes	Often	Always

7/ The rules constantly change dependent upon her/his mood.

1	2	3	4	5
Never	Rarely	Sometimes	Often	Always

8/ I do not know if I am breaking the rules because he/she does not tell me what they are.

1	2	3	4	5
Never	Rarely	Sometimes	Often	Always

9/ She/he makes contact with my family members before mentioning it to me.

1	2	3	4	5
Never	Rarely	Sometimes	Often	Always

10/ He/she makes contact with my friends before mentioning it to me.

1	2	3	4	5
Never	Rarely	Sometimes	Often	Always

11/ She/he makes contact with my work colleagues/other professionals before mentioning it to me.

1	2	3	4	5
Never	Rarely	Sometimes	Often	Always

12/ They (FP and my family/friends/work colleagues/other professionals) share inside jokes about my habits.

1	2	3	4	5
Never	Rarely	Sometimes	Often	Always

13/ They (FP and my family/friends/work colleagues/other professionals) share inside jokes about my faults.

1	2	3	4	5
Never	Rarely	Sometimes	Often	Always

14/ They (FP and my family/friends/work colleagues/other professionals) share inside jokes about my decisions.

1	2	3	4	5
Never	Rarely	Sometimes	Often	Always

15/ They (FP and my family/friends/work colleagues/other professionals) share inside jokes about my opinions.

1	2	3	4	5
Never	Rarely	Sometimes	Often	Always

16/ Their (FP's) sharing of inside jokes made about me makes me feel uncomfortable.

1	2	3	4	5
Never	Rarely	Sometimes	Often	Always

17/ She/he makes inappropriate jokes about me in front of me in public.

1	2	3	4	5
Never	Rarely	Sometimes	Often	Always

18/ He/she criticises me in front of other people.

1	2	3	4	5
Never	Rarely	Sometimes	Often	Always

19/ I am criticised by him/her especially when he/she is in a mood.

1	2	3	4	5
Never	Rarely	Sometimes	Often	Always

20/ After we have disagreements I receive a reward/gift (from FP).

1	2	3	4	5
Never	Rarely	Sometimes	Often	Always

21/ After he/she loses his/her temper I am given a gift/reward to make things better.

1	2	3	4	5
Never	Rarely	Sometimes	Often	Always

22/ I am told by him/her that that making decisions for me is because I am so loved.

1	2	3	4	5
Never	Rarely	Sometimes	Often	Always

23/ She/he vacillates between criticism of me and telling me that I am wonderful/the best/valued greatly.

1	2	3	4	5
Never	Rarely	Sometimes	Often	Always

24/ I receive big compliments between insults by her/him.

1	2	3	4	5
Never	Rarely	Sometimes	Often	Always

25/ I am expected to be available to him/her regardless of what I am doing at the time.

1	2	3	4	5
Never	Rarely	Sometimes	Often	Always

26/ I feel that he/she is rushing me into making the relationship long-term.

1	2	3	4	5
Never	Rarely	Sometimes	Often	Always

27/ He/she flirts with other women/men right infront of me.

1	2	3	4	5
Never	Rarely	Sometimes	Often	Always

28/ When I communicate that I am upset with her/his behaviors toward me she/he blames me.

1	2	3	4	5
Never	Rarely	Sometimes	Often	Always

29/ There is an expectation that I be grateful and thank him/her for time/gifts/rewards long after they have been received.

1	2	3	4	5
Never	Rarely	Sometimes	Often	Always

30/ I am made to feel that this is the only relationship/connection that I will ever have the opportunity to experience.

1	2	3	4	5
Never	Rarely	Sometimes	Often	Always

31/ I am becoming nervous that I am the cause when he/she becomes upset/loses his/her temper.

1	2	3	4	5
Never	Rarely	Sometimes	Often	Always

32/ I am starting to blame myself for problems in the relationship/connection.

1	2	3	4	5
Never	Rarely	Sometimes	Often	Always

33/ My likes seem secondary to his/her likes.

1	2	3	4	5
Never	Rarely	Sometimes	Often	Always

34/ My dislikes seem secondary to her/his dislikes.

1	2	3	4	5
Never	Rarely	Sometimes	Often	Always

35/ My views are dismissed in favour of his/her's.

1	2	3	4	5
Never	Rarely	Sometimes	Often	Always

36/ My opinions are dismissed in favour of her's/his.

1	2	3	4	5
Never	Rarely	Sometimes	Often	Always

37/ She/he tells me that she/he is protective because I am too sensitive and/or analytical.

1	2	3	4	5
Never	Rarely	Sometimes	Often	Always

------- GROOMING Subscale Score: ______________

<h1 style="text-align:center"><u>HOSTAGE to cruelty Subscale:</u></h1>

38/ When I plan my finances he/she blocks me and takes over.

1	2	3	4	5
Never	Rarely	Sometimes	Often	Always

39/ Every decision I make in her/his eyes is wrong and stupid.

1	2	3	4	5
Never	Rarely	Sometimes	Often	Always

40/ If I try to reason with him/her about important decisions I am ridiculed.

1	2	3	4	5
Never	Rarely	Sometimes	Often	Always

41/ She/he silences me when I try to help in a crisis situation.

1	2	3	4	5
Never	Rarely	Sometimes	Often	Always

42/ Delay tactics, including refusal to discuss difficult situations, occur in response to my concerns.

1	2	3	4	5
Never	Rarely	Sometimes	Often	Always

43/ I am not left alone, he/she is either in my physical presence or making contact with me.

1	2	3	4	5
Never	Rarely	Sometimes	Often	Always

44/ I am given set tasks which I must complete every day.

1	2	3	4	5
Never	Rarely	Sometimes	Often	Always

45/ My thoughts and feelings are not private, as I am required to divulge all to him/her.

1	2	3	4	5
Never	Rarely	Sometimes	Often	Always

46/ I am scared of his/her unpredictable behaviors.

1	2	3	4	5
Never	Rarely	Sometimes	Often	Always

47/ I am made a scapegoat for his/her problems.

1	2	3	4	5
Never	Rarely	Sometimes	Often	Always

48/ I am frightened of her/him when she/he loses their temper.

1	2	3	4	5
Never	Rarely	Sometimes	Often	Always

49/ When he/she is angry he/she gets in my face.

1	2	3	4	5
Never	Rarely	Sometimes	Often	Always

50/ When he/she is angry he/she screams, shouts and/or swears at me.

1	2	3	4	5
Never	Rarely	Sometimes	Often	Always

51/ When he/she is angry he/she makes verbal threats to my safety.

1	2	3	4	5
Never	Rarely	Sometimes	Often	Always

52/ When he/she is angry he/she grabs me and/or hits me and/or punches me.

1	2	3	4	5
Never	Rarely	Sometimes	Often	Always

53/ I am fearful of her/him day to day.

1	2	3	4	5
Never	Rarely	Sometimes	Often	Always

54/ A bad relationship/connection is my lot in life.

1	2	3	4	5
Never	Rarely	Sometimes	Often	Always

55/ I look forward to his/her company but fear it at the same time.

1	2	3	4	5
Never	Rarely	Sometimes	Often	Always

56/ I used to feel satisfied about being my own person but now I know that I need her/him to live.

1	2	3	4	5
Never	Rarely	Sometimes	Often	Always

57/ It is like 'us (FP and me) versus the rest of the world'.

1	2	3	4	5
Never	Rarely	Sometimes	Often	Always

58/ Some of my friends tell me that I have changed since being with him/her, and that they are worried.

1	2	3	4	5
Never	Rarely	Sometimes	Often	Always

59/ I do not have contact with many of my friends, since being with him/her.

1	2	3	4	5
Never	Rarely	Sometimes	Often	Always

60/ I do not have contact with much of my family, since being with him/her.

1	2	3	4	5
Never	Rarely	Sometimes	Often	Always

61/ I do not have contact with many of my work colleagues/other professionals, since being with her/him.

1	2	3	4	5
Never	Rarely	Sometimes	Often	Always

62/ We are so attached to each other it is hard to breathe.

1	2	3	4	5
Never	Rarely	Sometimes	Often	Always

63/ I feel compelled to join her/him even when she/he is doing something dangerous.

1	2	3	4	5
Never	Rarely	Sometimes	Often	Always

64/ I feel compelled to join him/her even when I know that others would see it as doing wrong.

1	2	3	4	5
Never	Rarely	Sometimes	Often	Always

65/ If he/she understands me then I must understand him/her.

1	2	3	4	5
Never	Rarely	Sometimes	Often	Always

66/ When she/he hurts me I feel sorry for her/him.

1	2	3	4	5
Never	Rarely	Sometimes	Often	Always

67/ Despite my fear, he/she is a good person at heart.

1	2	3	4	5
Never	Rarely	Sometimes	Often	Always

68/ I am lucky to be in this relationship/connection.

1	2	3	4	5
Never	Rarely	Sometimes	Often	Always

69/ I am too ungrateful.

1	2	3	4	5
Never	Rarely	Sometimes	Often	Always

70/ I am aware that I am crazy.

1	2	3	4	5
Never	Rarely	Sometimes	Often	Always

71/ I know that I am stupid.

1	2	3	4	5
Never	Rarely	Sometimes	Often	Always

72/ I am nothing without him/her telling me what to do.

1	2	3	4	5
Never	Rarely	Sometimes	Often	Always

73/ I am nothing without her/him telling me how to think and what to believe.

1	2	3	4	5
Never	Rarely	Sometimes	Often	Always

74/ I am reliant on him/her to meet my basic needs (food, water, housing, health).

1	2	3	4	5
Never	Rarely	Sometimes	Often	Always

75/ He/she used to give me gifts, now I feel rewarded when he/she is not showing anger towards me.

1	2	3	4	5
Never	Rarely	Sometimes	Often	Always

76/ He/she makes me feel in danger.

1	2	3	4	5
Never	Rarely	Sometimes	Often	Always

77/ I try hard to be a good girl/good boy to please her/him.

1	2	3	4	5
Never	Rarely	Sometimes	Often	Always

78/ I apologise for being me every day.

1	2	3	4	5
Never	Rarely	Sometimes	Often	Always

79/ It is my fault when he/she becomes nasty.

1	2	3	4	5
Never	Rarely	Sometimes	Often	Always

80/ I am the guilty person in the relationship/connection.

1	2	3	4	5
Never	Rarely	Sometimes	Often	Always

81/ I am the cause of all the problems within the relationship/connection.

1	2	3	4	5
Never	Rarely	Sometimes	Often	Always

82/ When she/he threatens to leave/disconnect from me I start panicking.

1	2	3	4	5
Never	Rarely	Sometimes	Often	Always

83/ To be rejected is the worst thing in the world.

1	2	3	4	5
Never	Rarely	Sometimes	Often	Always

84/ I have thoughts that I am becoming even more insane.

1	2	3	4	5
Never	Rarely	Sometimes	Often	Always

85/ Part of being crazy, is that I imagine things (according to the FP).

1	2	3	4	5
Never	Rarely	Sometimes	Often	Always

86/ He/she says that my friend and/or work colleagues/other professionals only pretend to like me.

1	2	3	4	5
Never	Rarely	Sometimes	Often	Always

87/ He/she becomes confused and forgetful about any upsetting incidences between us.

1	2	3	4	5
Never	Rarely	Sometimes	Often	Always

88/ The (FP) calls me a liar, even though I am not one.

1	2	3	4	5
Never	Rarely	Sometimes	Often	Always

89/ She/he likes secrecy, and I am expected to adhere to this.

1	2	3	4	5
Never	Rarely	Sometimes	Often	Always

----------HOSTAGE to cruelty Subscale Score______________

<u>FRAGMENTATION Subscale:</u>

90/ There is nothing I can do to get myself out of the situation (relationship/connection).

1	2	3	4	5
Never	Rarely	Sometimes	Often	Always

91/ I agreed to start the relationship/connection so it is my fault how it turned out.

1	2	3	4	5
Never	Rarely	Sometimes	Often	Always

92/ I am nothing, now.

1	2	3	4	5
Never	Rarely	Sometimes	Often	Always

93/ I am a shell of a person.

1	2	3	4	5
Never	Rarely	Sometimes	Often	Always

94/ I used to have my own thoughts and ideas but now I cannot think without him/her.

1	2	3	4	5
Never	Rarely	Sometimes	Often	Always

95/ I hate who I have become.

1	2	3	4	5
Never	Rarely	Sometimes	Often	Always

96/ I feel completely emotionally drained.

1	2	3	4	5
Never	Rarely	Sometimes	Often	Always

97/ I feel totally physically exhausted.

1	2	3	4	5
Never	Rarely	Sometimes	Often	Always

98/ I have not trusted my gut feelings/intuition since committing to this relationship/connection.

1	2	3	4	5
Never	Rarely	Sometimes	Often	Always

99/ I hide all my problems from others, aside from him/her.

1	2	3	4	5
Never	Rarely	Sometimes	Often	Always

100/ I choose not to go out unless absolutely necessary, or only go when he/she tells me to.

1	2	3	4	5
Never	Rarely	Sometimes	Often	Always

101/ Everyone I know (aside from FP) tells me things like: that I have changed so much that they do not recognize who I have become.

1	2	3	4	5
Never	Rarely	Sometimes	Often	Always

102/ I thought that I was mad before, but now I know it through and through.

1	2	3	4	5
Never	Rarely	Sometimes	Often	Always

103/ I know that I am a burden on her/him and feel guilty because of it.

1	2	3	4	5
Never	Rarely	Sometimes	Often	Always

104/ My complete world consists of me and him/her.

1	2	3	4	5
Never	Rarely	Sometimes	Often	Always

105/ I feel detached from the world outside of me and him/her.

1	2	3	4	5
Never	Rarely	Sometimes	Often	Always

106/ I have no interest in relating or connecting with others outside of my world.

1	2	3	4	5
Never	Rarely	Sometimes	Often	Always

107/ Others' (aside from the FP's) problems and feelings are not my concern.

1	2	3	4	5
Never	Rarely	Sometimes	Often	Always

108/ I used to care for all others, and give so much to others.

1	2	3	4	5
Never	Rarely	Sometimes	Often	Always

109/ I have no sense of purpose other than pleasing him/her.

1	2	3	4	5
Never	Rarely	Sometimes	Often	Always

110/ My professionalism in my work has suffered since my interactions with her/him.

1	2	3	4	5
Never	Rarely	Sometimes	Often	Always

111/ In the past I held personal integrity in high regard, now people can do what they want 'I don't care'.

1	2	3	4	5
Never	Rarely	Sometimes	Often	Always

112/ Ethical standards only apply to those who are in a position to exercise them.

1	2	3	4	5
Never	Rarely	Sometimes	Often	Always

113/ I am so confused that I do not know what my standards are anymore.

1	2	3	4	5
Never	Rarely	Sometimes	Often	Always

114/ My true self is defined day to day dependent upon his/her demands.

1	2	3	4	5
Never	Rarely	Sometimes	Often	Always

115/ He/she would say that morality is for fools.

1	2	3	4	5
Never	Rarely	Sometimes	Often	Always

116/ I feel shame and regret.

1	2	3	4	5
Never	Rarely	Sometimes	Often	Always

117/ I am made to feel guilty for everything.

1	2	3	4	5
Never	Rarely	Sometimes	Often	Always

118/ He/she must be right, I am over dramatising the situation that I am in.

1	2	3	4	5
Never	Rarely	Sometimes	Often	Always

----------FRAGMENTATION Subscale Score_______________

<u>revelationary SHOCK Subscale:</u>

119/ I am capable of recognising abuse of others, because of my own experience with abuse.

1	2	3	4	5
Never	Rarely	Sometimes	Often	Always

120/ I now recognise that I am/ have been a victim of abuse.

1	2	3	4	5
Never	Rarely	Sometimes	Often	Always

121/ I am aware of the term gaslighting, and that it relates to my experience.

1	2	3	4	5
Never	Rarely	Sometimes	Often	Always

122/ I have been/am a victim of gaslighting.

1	2	3	4	5
Never	Rarely	Sometimes	Often	Always

123/ My hands shake and/or I feel jumpy.

1	2	3	4	5
Never	Rarely	Sometimes	Often	Always

124/ My whole body shakes.

1	2	3	4	5
Never	Rarely	Sometimes	Often	Always

125/ I feel so shaky that my insides shake as well.

1	2	3	4	5
Never	Rarely	Sometimes	Often	Always

126/ I feel physically numb.

1	2	3	4	5
Never	Rarely	Sometimes	Often	Always

127/ I cannot think straight.

1	2	3	4	5
Never	Rarely	Sometimes	Often	Always

128/ His/her toxic words and actions are at the forefront of my thoughts.

1	2	3	4	5
Never	Rarely	Sometimes	Often	Always

129/ I can see that he/she behaves in toxic ways.

1	2	3	4	5
Never	Rarely	Sometimes	Often	Always

130/ I know that she/he directs toxic words and behaviors towards me.

1	2	3	4	5
Never	Rarely	Sometimes	Often	Always

131/ I am aware that I am his/her primary target of control.

1	2	3	4	5
Never	Rarely	Sometimes	Often	Always

132/ I am stunned by the realisation that I am/have been gaslighted/abused.

1	2	3	4	5
Never	Rarely	Sometimes	Often	Always

133/ I cannot talk much about my feelings and reactions (to the realisation that I am/have been gaslighted/abused).

1	2	3	4	5
Never	Rarely	Sometimes	Often	Always

134/ I cannot stop talking about my feelings and reactions (to the realisation that I am/have been gaslighted/abused).

1	2	3	4	5
Never	Rarely	Sometimes	Often	Always

135/ I am anxious about remaining a victim of gaslighting abuse.

1	2	3	4	5
Never	Rarely	Sometimes	Often	Always

136/ I would do anything to make him/her stop.

1	2	3	4	5
Never	Rarely	Sometimes	Often	Always

137/ Maybe if I just tell her/him to stop behaving badly toward me she/he will.

1	2	3	4	5
Never	Rarely	Sometimes	Often	Always

138/ Not everything has been my fault throughout the relationship/connection, but alot was.

1	2	3	4	5
Never	Rarely	Sometimes	Often	Always

139/ I recognise some of the ways in which (the FP) has/had power over me.

1	2	3	4	5
Never	Rarely	Sometimes	Often	Always

140/ He/she is cruel.

1	2	3	4	5
Never	Rarely	Sometimes	Often	Always

141/ She/he is to blame for the abuse/gaslighting which I/have endure(d), but I still blame myself.

1	2	3	4	5
Never	Rarely	Sometimes	Often	Always

142/ I feel betrayed by him/her.

1	2	3	4	5
Never	Rarely	Sometimes	Often	Always

143/ I am able to provide clear examples of the abuse/gaslighting which I have suffered.

1	2	3	4	5
Never	Rarely	Sometimes	Often	Always

144/ I was not imagining the gaslighting/abuse.

1	2	3	4	5
Never	Rarely	Sometimes	Often	Always

145/ I feel crazy with shock and fear, but am coming to understand that I am not actually crazy.

1	2	3	4	5
Never	Rarely	Sometimes	Often	Always

146/ I want to escape from the relationship/connection now.

1	2	3	4	5
Never	Rarely	Sometimes	Often	Always

147/ I have thought of ways to escape (from the FP).

1	2	3	4	5
Never	Rarely	Sometimes	Often	Always

148/ I fear that I need outside help to make myself safe.

1	2	3	4	5
Never	Rarely	Sometimes	Often	Always

149/ I have made definite plans to leave the situation.

1	2	3	4	5
Never	Rarely	Sometimes	Often	Always

150/ I am aware that my personal standards have been compromised.

1	2	3	4	5
Never	Rarely	Sometimes	Often	Always

151/ I know that my morals have changed as a result of the relationship/connection.

1	2	3	4	5
Never	Rarely	Sometimes	Often	Always

-------revelationary SHOCK Subscale Score________________

<u>AFTERMATH Subscale:</u>

152/ I feel so betrayed by him/her that my anger is unbearable.

1	2	3	4	5
Never	Rarely	Sometimes	Often	Always

153/ My disgust for what he/she has done to me is barely contained.

1	2	3	4	5
Never	Rarely	Sometimes	Often	Always

154/ I find it hard to forgive my family members (non-FP) for playing along with her/him.

1	2	3	4	5
Never	Rarely	Sometimes	Often	Always

155/ I find it hard to forgive my friends (non-FP) for playing along with him/her.

1	2	3	4	5
Never	Rarely	Sometimes	Often	Always

156/ I find it hard to forgive trusted others (non-FP) for playing along with him/her.

1	2	3	4	5
Never	Rarely	Sometimes	Often	Always

157/ Her/his betrayal runs so deep that my relationships/connections with others has been damaged.

1	2	3	4	5
Never	Rarely	Sometimes	Often	Always

158/ I avoid intimacy (in relationships/connections) with others.

1	2	3	4	5
Never	Rarely	Sometimes	Often	Always

159/ I crave intimacy with others, and pursued another relationship/connection immediately after I left him/her.

1	2	3	4	5
Never	Rarely	Sometimes	Often	Always

160/ I avoid social interactions.

1	2	3	4	5
Never	Rarely	Sometimes	Often	Always

161/ I avoid all reminders of the her/him and the situation that I was in.

1	2	3	4	5
Never	Rarely	Sometimes	Often	Always

162/ I feel sickened at the thoughts of my gaslighting abuse experiences.

1	2	3	4	5
Never	Rarely	Sometimes	Often	Always

163/ All the things he/she used to say, and do, go round and round in my head.

1	2	3	4	5
Never	Rarely	Sometimes	Often	Always

164/ There are so many things which remind me of her/him and/or the gaslighting abuse.

1	2	3	4	5
Never	Rarely	Sometimes	Often	Always

165/ I have difficulty focussing on tasks at hand and/or decision making.

1	2	3	4	5
Never	Rarely	Sometimes	Often	Always

166/ I have nightmares about the situation that I was in.

1	2	3	4	5
Never	Rarely	Sometimes	Often	Always

167/ I have problems sleeping.

1	2	3	4	5
Never	Rarely	Sometimes	Often	Always

168/ I sleep alot.

1	2	3	4	5
Never	Rarely	Sometimes	Often	Always

169/ I experience periods when I am unaware of time and place, whilst thinking of the gaslighting abuse.

1	2	3	4	5
Never	Rarely	Sometimes	Often	Always

170/ Others tell me that I have times when I appear to zone out and become incommunicable.

1	2	3	4	5
Never	Rarely	Sometimes	Often	Always

171/ I am anxious.

1	2	3	4	5
Never	Rarely	Sometimes	Often	Always

172/ I am depressed.

1	2	3	4	5
Never	Rarely	Sometimes	Often	Always

173/ When I am among strangers (eg in a public place), I feel like everyone who looks at me knows exactly what I have been through.

1	2	3	4	5
Never	Rarely	Sometimes	Often	Always

174/ Everyone thinks that I am weak.

1	2	3	4	5
Never	Rarely	Sometimes	Often	Always

175/ Everyone thinks that I am mad.

1	2	3	4	5
Never	Rarely	Sometimes	Often	Always

176/ Noone believes me about what I have been through.

1	2	3	4	5
Never	Rarely	Sometimes	Often	Always

177/ People around me dismiss the concept of gaslighting and/or abuse.

1	2	3	4	5
Never	Rarely	Sometimes	Often	Always

178/ I am concerned that everyone will think that I am undeserving of a fulfilling life.

1	2	3	4	5
Never	Rarely	Sometimes	Often	Always

179/ I experience times when I believe that I am a bad person.

1	2	3	4	5
Never	Rarely	Sometimes	Often	Always

180/ I experience times when I think that I deserve what he/she did to me.

1	2	3	4	5
Never	Rarely	Sometimes	Often	Always

181/ I experience times when I think that I have been deservedly punished by her/him.

1	2	3	4	5
Never	Rarely	Sometimes	Often	Always

182/ I know that I tried my best (in the relationship/connection), but it did not work.

1	2	3	4	5
Never	Rarely	Sometimes	Often	Always

183/ I do not trust anyone.

1	2	3	4	5
Never	Rarely	Sometimes	Often	Always

184/ I am suspicious of others, when they treat me with respect and/or kindness.

1	2	3	4	5
Never	Rarely	Sometimes	Often	Always

185/ I take to heart anything negative said by others, and strike them off my (future interaction) list.

1	2	3	4	5
Never	Rarely	Sometimes	Often	Always

186/ I have no idea about what I can do to improve things for myself in the future.

1	2	3	4	5
Never	Rarely	Sometimes	Often	Always

187/ I used to pride myself upon professionalism, now it is just survival day to day.

1	2	3	4	5
Never	Rarely	Sometimes	Often	Always

188/ My integrity toward others was always (pre-FP) intact, now I just go with 'what is'- without getting involved.

1	2	3	4	5
Never	Rarely	Sometimes	Often	Always

189/ Ethical stances on situations are admirable, but I do not have the capacity to take an ethical stance on any issue.

1	2	3	4	5
Never	Rarely	Sometimes	Often	Always

190/ Feeling like a 'shell of a person' is an understatement in my personal situation.

1	2	3	4	5
Never	Rarely	Sometimes	Often	Always

191/ I used to consider myself a moral person, now I turn a 'blind eye' to everything as well as endorsing it.

1	2	3	4	5
Never	Rarely	Sometimes	Often	Always

192/ He/she used to tell me things like that I was morally corrupt and/or had no morals, now I wonder if he/she was telling me the truth.

1	2	3	4	5
Never	Rarely	Sometimes	Often	Always

193/ I am vulnerable to all walks of society.

1	2	3	4	5
Never	Rarely	Sometimes	Often	Always

194/ I feel vulnerable when talking about gaslighting.

1	2	3	4	5
Never	Rarely	Sometimes	Often	Always

195/ Although I feel vulnerable talking about myself, I know that it is necessary.

1	2	3	4	5
Never	Rarely	Sometimes	Often	Always

---------AFTERMATH Subscale Score________________

SUBSCALE	GVQ RAW SCORE	HIGH SCORE/RED FLAGS' ITEMS (undertake risk assessment or immediate intervention as per required)	GVQ MEAN SCORE
GROOMING			
HOSTAGE to cruelty			
FRAGMENTATION			
revelationary SHOCK			
AFTERMATH			
TOTAL SCORE (all relevant subscales summed)			

<h1 style="text-align:center"><u>Scoring:</u></h1>

<u>**Subscale Stage 1: Grooming:**</u>

Max score for subscale= 185

37 items total.

Score Ranges for this subscale:

High: 144-185

Moderate: 102-143

Low: 37-101

Calculate mean/average, accordingly.

<u>**Subscale Stage 2: Hostage to cruelty:**</u>

Max score for subscale= 260

52 items total

Score ranges for this subscale:

High: 200-260

Moderate: 76-199

Low: 52-75

Calculate mean/average, accordingly.

<u>Subscale Stage 3: Fragmentation:</u>

Max score for subscale= 145

29 items total

Score ranges for this subscale:

High: 112-145

Moderate: 46- 111

Low: 29- 45

Calculate mean/average, accordingly.

<u>Subscale Stage 4: revelationary Shock:</u>

Max score for subscale= 165

33 items total

Score ranges for this subscale:

High: 117- 165

Moderate: 53- 116

Low: 33- 52

Calculate mean/average, accordingly.

Subscale Stage 5: Aftermath:

Max score for subscale= 220

44 items total

Score ranges for this subscale:

High: 170- 220

Moderate: 71- 169

Low: 44- 70

Calculate mean/average, accordingly.

Not generally recommended, but for total score parameters of the GVQ scale (re-scaled summation)

Total max score= 975

High: 743- 975

Moderate: 344- 742

Low: 195- 343.

Calculate mean/average, accordingly.

<u>**Gaslighting Victims' Questionnaire (GVQ) Section 2 (Interview):**</u>

It is to be administered by healthcare, and allied healthcare professionals; and, qualified workers in domestic violence; human resources/occupational departments or outreach from such; patient safety, and ethics, professionals; trauma specialists; and, family support workers.

The GVQ is appropriate for 18 years or over (with a literacy level- verbal comprehension skills- of at least 15 years of age).

Clarification of any red flags' alert responses given in the 1st section of the GVQ questionnaire, to be undertaken.

As in, *"what are the reasons for rating .....(red flags- relevant subscale items) so highly?"*

Risk assessment to be undertaken, and immediate intervention/s to be put in place- as necessary.

1/ **"What was your upbringing like?"**

2/ **"Who were the major figures/influences/inspirations during your childhood and pre-adolescent periods of life?"**

3/ **"When did you experience your first significant friendship? Please describe what it was like. Please tell me about any difficult experiences with friendships, either currently or in the past"**

4/ **"When did you experience your first intimate relationship? Tell me about significant issues, of relevance, in intimate relationships beyond your first intimate relationship. Please tell me the primary details."**

5/ "What was your first job experience like? and subsequent ones?"

6/ "What is your current work status? Describe your interactions between managers and
co-workers."

7/ "At which age did you experience a significant interaction with a medical professional or with healthcare
(in general)?

Have you experienced any relevant negative interactions?
Provide details of the reasons for, and result of, the interaction/s."

8/ "Are you currently in a relationship with an intimate partner?"

9/ "If so, how does this partner treat you?"

10/ "How close are you to the members of your family? Please provide details of any significant issues."

11/ "Do you have interaction with your parents? What is the relationship like?"

12/ "What is your understanding of gaslighting and abuse?"

13/ "When did your suspicions about being gaslighted begin?"

14/ "Is the suspected gaslighting still continuing?"

15/ "How long do you feel that you have been suffering the effects from this?"

16/ "Or, when and how did it end?"

17/ "Have you ever suffered other gaslighting in the past (different FP)?"

18/ "If so, please explain what occured, the timeline, how you reacted, and if there was a lasting impact."

19/ "This is a standard question which is asked during administration of questionnaires:

Have you ever been diagnosed with a mental health issue?"

20/ "If so, when, by whom, and what is the condition/disorder with which you have been diagnosed?"

Additional question: "Is there anything related to your circumstances, feelings, behaviors, thoughts, or plans, which you feel I need to know about?"

Gaslighting Victims' Questionnaire- Short form (GVQ- Short form) Assessment Guidelines

The assessor is naturally expected to have gathered some relevant information about current and historical circumstances, beyond basic personal details- from the client/respondent- prior to the administration of the GVQ- Short form.

Assessor eligibility:

The GVQ- Short form is to be administered by healthcare, and allied healthcare professionals; and, suitably qualified workers in: domestic violence; human resources/occupational departments or outreach from such; patient safety, and ethics, professionals; trauma specialists; and, family support workers.

Respondent/ Client age range:

The GVQ-Short form is appropriate for administration to persons 18 years of age or over
(with a literacy level- verbal comprehension skills- of ages 15 years or over).

GVQ- Short form basic details:

It consists of 25 items (based on the 5 M.D. Tophus GHFSA stages:
Grooming; Hostage to cruelty; Fragmentation; revelationary Shock; and, Aftermath).

<u>**Suitability for Gaslighting types:**</u>

-intimate partnerships (domestic)

-familial

-parental

-work/occupational

-medical

-healthcare environments.

Thus, it is a questionnaire suited to reflect gaslighting in a wide variety of circumstances and environments. For instance, in the case of medical gaslighting, this may correlate with existing transference and counter-transference issues, between patient/client and medical professional/therapist.

<u>**Respondent/client focus:**</u>

When there are multiple identified gaslighters involved, it is necessary for the victim to choose the most extensive of the gaslighters, or a repeat of the questionnaire must be undertaken per key gaslighter.

In the event of history of gaslighting in for example- multiple intimate partnerships, then the victim is required to focus only upon the key gaslighter- the alleged perpetrator in question.

<u>**Process of administering the GVQ- Short form:**</u>

Upon introducing the administration of the GVQ- Short form, the assessor is to give a brief description of gaslighting to the respondent
(please refer to M.D. Tophus' 'Gaslighting' publication for more), without providing extensive examples of such.

<u>**Clarification of key words:**</u>

The Focal Person, referred to in the questionnaires as 'FP', typically may be an
intimate partner, parent, family member, work colleague/manager, healthcare professional, or other professional.

<u>**Extraneous respondent/client variables for consideration:**</u>

Much is dependent upon the stage of gaslighting victimisation: is it current,
or are they in 'freeze' mode- prolonged hostage to cruelty, or fragmentation, stages or attending in the stage of revelationary shock- about to leave, or after the fact- the aftermath?.

In relation to extraneous variables, there is also the issue of a respondent's traumatic memory loss, detachment, or dissociative issues. These can affect memory and cause memory deficit (either temporary, or otherwise). So too, with level of respondent insight into perpetrations of gaslighting.
Client disclosure of previously diagnosed conditions, along with the assessor's observation skills, and professional intuition, may elicit this as a consideration.

Some questions are included specifically to ensure consistency and reliability of responses provided.

<u>**Additional recommended assessment/s:**</u>

Assessment for pre-existing clinical disorders, which may impact the results of the questionnaire
is recommended in some cases. This is also relevant for the GVQ.

Assessment for Acute Stress Disorder, or Post-Traumatic Stress Disorder, may also be necessary following
administration of either the GVQ- Short form, or the GVQ.

<u>**Scoring and results:**</u>

Lower scores (non-red/yellow flags), do not necessarily mean that the victim is sans:
current suffering or not in imminent danger. There are multiple variables which can influence a victim's
rating of the statements included in the questionnaire. The importance of experienced, qualified
administrators comes into play as professional prowess requires efficient utilisation of the results.

<u>**During administration of the GVQ Short form, the assessor is required to place a mark/notation for their
immediate reference, against any responses given which triggers a red flag alert.**</u>

<u>**(A 'red flag' is considered to be anything which indicates harm to self or others- including potential for).**</u>

**The assessor may then ask for specific clarification (regarding the red flags' alert responses provided)
from the respondent immediately following having administered the questionnaire.**

A risk assessment and/or immediate intervention, is essential- as per required.

<u>**Gaslighting Victims' Questionnaire- Short form (GVQ-Short form)**</u>

The Gaslighting Victims' Questionnaire- Short form: GVQ- Short form has 25 items adapted from the GVQ.
It is based on the M.D. Tophus' 5 Stages of Victims'Gaslighting. The short form incorporates primary gaslighting abuse elements of: manipulation; control; labelling; intrusive cognitions; self-esteem; hostage like symptomatology; fear-mongering; and symptoms of gaslighting impact.

It is to be administered by healthcare, and allied healthcare professionals; and, suitably qualified workers in: domestic violence; human resources/occupational departments or outreach from such; patient safety, and ethics, professionals; trauma specialists; and, family support workers.

The GVQ- Short form is appropriate for 18 years or over (with a literacy level- verbal comprehension skills of at least 15 years of age).

<u>**During administration of the GVQ Short form, the assessor is required to place a mark/notation for their immediate reference, against any responses given which triggers a red flag alert.**</u>

<u>**(A 'red flag' is considered to be anything which indicates harm to self or others- including potential for).**</u>

The assessor may then ask for specific clarification (regarding the red flags' alert responses provided) from the respondent immediately following having administered the questionnaire.

A risk assessment and/or immediate intervention, is essential- as per required.

Please provide the client with the 1-5 rating response scale for visual prompting.

Assessor to say to the respondent:
"Please focus your thoughts and responses on the key person identified, this is referred to as the FP: the focal person, or person of focus"

<u>**Gaslighting Victims' Questionnaire- Short form (GVQ-Short form) Scale**</u>

The GVQ-Short form is to be administered by healthcare, and allied healthcare professionals; and, qualified workers in domestic violence; human resources/occupational departments or outreach from such; patient safety, and ethics, professionals; trauma specialists; and, family support workers.

The GVQ is appropriate for 18 years or over (with a literacy level- verbal comprehension skills-
of at least 15 years of age).

NAME of CLIENT	
CLIENT'S Date of Birth	
DATE ADMINISTERED	
NAME of ASSESSOR	
ASSESSOR'S RECOMMENDATIONS for FURTHER ASSESSMENT MEASURES/IMMEDIATE INTERVENTION(S)	

1/ I do not know if I am breaking the rules because he/she does not tell me what they are.

1	2	3	4	5
Never	Rarely	Sometimes	Often	Always

2/ I am not left alone, he/she is either in my physical presence or making contact with me.

1	2	3	4	5
Never	Rarely	Sometimes	Often	Always

3/ I am made to feel that this is the only relationship/connection that I will ever have the opportunity to experience.

1	2	3	4	5
Never	Rarely	Sometimes	Often	Always

4/ When she/he is angry she/he makes verbal threats to my safety.

1	2	3	4	5
Never	Rarely	Sometimes	Often	Always

5/ I am fearful of him/her day to day.

1	2	3	4	5
Never	Rarely	Sometimes	Often	Always

6/ I used to feel satisfied about being my own person but now I know that I need her/him to live.

1	2	3	4	5
Never	Rarely	Sometimes	Often	Always

7/ It is like 'us (FP and me) versus the rest of the world'.

1	2	3	4	5
Never	Rarely	Sometimes	Often	Always

8/ To be rejected is the worst thing in the world.

1	2	3	4	5
Never	Rarely	Sometimes	Often	Always

9/ Part of being crazy, is that I imagine things (according to the FP).

1	2	3	4	5
Never	Rarely	Sometimes	Often	Always

10/ It is my fault when he/she becomes nasty.

1	2	3	4	5
Never	Rarely	Sometimes	Often	Always

11/ I am a shell of a person.

1	2	3	4	5
Never	Rarely	Sometimes	Often	Always

12/ I choose not to go out unless absolutely necessary, or only go when he/she tells me to.

1	2	3	4	5
Never	Rarely	Sometimes	Often	Always

13/ My true self is defined, day to day, dependent upon his/her demands.

1	2	3	4	5
Never	Rarely	Sometimes	Often	Always

14/ I feel shame and regret.

1	2	3	4	5
Never	Rarely	Sometimes	Often	Always

15/ I am aware of the term gaslighting, and that it relates to my experience.

1	2	3	4	5
Never	Rarely	Sometimes	Often	Always

16/ My hands shake and/or I feel jumpy.

1	2	3	4	5
Never	Rarely	Sometimes	Often	Always

17/ Her/his toxic words are at the forefront of my thoughts.

1	2	3	4	5
Never	Rarely	Sometimes	Often	Always

18/ I am aware that I am his/her primary target of control.

1	2	3	4	5
Never	Rarely	Sometimes	Often	Always

19/ I would do anything to make him/her stop.

1	2	3	4	5
Never	Rarely	Sometimes	Often	Always

20/ She/he is cruel.

1	2	3	4	5
Never	Rarely	Sometimes	Often	Always

21/ I feel betrayed by him/her.

1	2	3	4	5
Never	Rarely	Sometimes	Often	Always

22/ I experience periods when I am unaware of time and place, whilst thinking of the gaslighting abuse.

1	2	3	4	5
Never	Rarely	Sometimes	Often	Always

23/ Everyone thinks that I am weak.

1	2	3	4	5
Never	Rarely	Sometimes	Often	Always

24/ I experience times when I think that I have been deservedly punished by him/her.

1	2	3	4	5
Never	Rarely	Sometimes	Often	Always

25/ I am vulnerable to all walks of society.

1	2	3	4	5
Never	Rarely	Sometimes	Often	Always

<u>Scoring:</u>

High: 100- 125

Moderate: 51- 99

Low: 25- 50

Calculate the mean/average, accordingly.

GVQ- Short form RAW SCORE	GVQ- Short form MEAN SCORE	RED FLAGS' ALERT Notations (undertake risk assessment or immediate intervention as per required)

REFERENCES

(1) Tophus, M.D. Gaslighting, Germany: Hilphma Publications, p.9.

www.ingramcontent.com/pod-product-compliance
Lightning Source LLC
Chambersburg PA
CBHW070905260726
48661CB00004B/1601